How to Create the Ultimate Wedding Planning Binder
And other helpful wedding planning tips

Heather Waugh

TABLE OF CONTENTS

Preface

When I got engaged, I was beyond ecstatic. After two days of telling everyone and showing off my ring, I panicked. Not because I was suddenly afraid of commitment, it was the realization that I knew nothing about wedding planning.

Since I had no experience with weddings, I felt overwhelmed and rushed to set a date that would give me plenty of time to learn. I knew I wanted to get married in the autumn, but I was engaged mid-January and felt that the coming fall was too soon. So I set the date two and a half years away. That was a *big* mistake.

After a week of hard research, I understood how simple planning a wedding is no matter what the time frame. All I needed was organization. I chose to make a wedding binder to prepare for all of the tasks ahead of me. This binder (which I had affectionately nicknamed The Monstrosity by the time the wedding day arrived) was full of facts, advice, brainstorming, budgeting, receipts, official details, and more. Every vendor I met was very impressed and loved the fact I was more prepared than most of their clients, to the point where I was beating their own professional planning systems. Past and fellow brides told me they wished they had outlined a timeline with details like I did, that it would have made their engagement period way less stressful. These comments indicated there was a need for a wedding planning organization system such as mine.

This book is to show every bride how easy it is to plan a wedding regardless how much time you have. I will outline step-by-step how to construct and manage your binder and guide you through timing, tasks, and tips that will save you time, stress, and money. Being organized will make your engagement and planning time more enjoyable and less stressful.

The Essentials: Setting a Date, Timeline, and Gathering Supplies

Before any planning can begin, the wedding date needs to be set. For me, this was the most drama-weighted part of planning. Speak with your fiancé and talk about your lives, your work, and your timelines. This could be the difference between a date set three months from now or three years from now.

TIP: *When I say "set a date," it does not have to be exact. Instead, pick the month and year you want to get married. You and your fiancé can have a preference for the day of the week and date, but when booking you may not be able to get it. Vendor and venue availability will set the official date.*

Don't get upset if after discussing the date with your fiancé, you need to have a whole wedding planned in a couple of months. Whatever your timeframe, the wedding of your dreams *will* happen if you stay organized and on a strict timeline.

The reason I don't suggest setting an actual date is because of the vendors. Whether you are on a short or long timeline (especially if you are on a shorter timeline), prioritize what is most important to you. For example, if there is a particular photographer you *have* to have, then contact them first for their availability, book the best day they offer, then ask other vendors for that date. Not every place will be available on the same day. This is why it is important to decide what is the highest priority to you. For other vendors and venues, research options and make lists of your top three to five favorites, all of which should go into your Vendor section of the wedding binder. Contact all of them to check their availability to see if it matches the date you reserved with your favorite vendor.

TIP: The most traditional day to get married is a Saturday. However, there is more availability from vendors on Friday and Sunday. Usually vendors offer cheaper rates for booking on these days due to lower demand. If nothing is working out on a Saturday, consider a Friday or Sunday, or, if you're nontraditional and want better date selection and rates, choose a Monday through Thursday.

After the date, outline a timeline based on how many months (or weeks) you have to plan. When you don't know a thing about planning a wedding, creating a timeline can be daunting. Basically, begin researching immediately where you want to get married and have the reception. Additionally, research all the vendors you may want to hire for your wedding. Booking these places and people will be the first step on your timeline. Next, think about the invitations, décor, dress, accessories, marriage license, gift registration, and other wedding celebrations leading up to the day. All of this will be covered in the rest of the book.

For now, calculate how many months you have to plan. Divide these up into two to three month segments if you have more time to plan. The timeline is broken down by month once at the three month mark until the big day. Six weeks before, the timeline needs to be weekly. The week of the wedding, plan your tasks daily. Trust me, your days will be filled.

It is important to remember that life happens. The timeline is an estimated guide. You may get things done a month earlier than its due date or complete things that due six months ago the day before the wedding. No matter what, everything that needs to get done will get done once you write it down. The timeline is just an ideal guide to help outline the process.

The budget is a consideration when planning your date and timeline. I found it easier to set an overall idea of the type of wedding I could afford rather than an actual dollar amount. No matter what you plan and budget, you are *always* going to exceed your spending limit. I was on a tight, frugal budget and could not finalize a spending limit or accurately estimate how much the entire wedding would cost. Instead, I prioritized what I could splurge on and what had to be as cheap as possible. I saved a lot of money and still had my perfect wedding without crying over bills later.

TIP: *I know this is hard, but try to pay everything for the wedding with cash or a debit card. Putting things on a credit card will leave you with post-wedding payments that weigh you down. Paying for your one special day after it's over is depressing and makes the memory of the day lose its magic. If necessary to charge some of the expense try limiting to only the honeymoon. If a credit card is used, it is advised to outline a payment plan so the debt is paid before the wedding day.*

After the timeline section of your binder, plan your ideal budget and spending track, including your priority to splurge list. However, I wouldn't obsess over it too much since you are going to blow it anyway. Every couple does.

Now to the most important part of your planning – the binder. A three ring binder, of any size, will suffice. In hindsight, I should have used a two inch binder so I could easily add and remove paper. Purchase dividers for the different sections you will be planning.

TIP: *Use 3-hole punched folders instead of basic dividers. This allows you to put receipts, business cards, and other important scraps of paper in their appropriate categorized folder.*

To start, buy ten dividers or folders. The sections for these dividers will be labeled:

To-Do List and Budget
Guest Lists and Invitations
Ceremony
Reception
Décor
Vendors
Dress and Bridal Party Outfits
Beauty
Registry and Gift Track
Honeymoon

Feel free to break these folders apart or combine them together. If one of the sections is more important to you than others (such as if you have a ton of ideas for the centerpieces that is overtaking your décor folder, make centerpieces its own folder). For the remainder of this book, however, I will be referencing the folders in this order. There will be other miscellaneous things you can add to these folders, or you can include more for extra categories. The most important thing about your binder is that *you* understand how it's organized. My list is only a suggested guide.

The binder should contain pens or pencils to scribble notes during meetings or while brainstorming at home. The information contained within can be typed and then printed or simply hand written on notebook paper. I preferred notebook paper because it was easier to take notes from websites and I could instantly put the information in my binder. There were some things I printed, such as receipts, reservations, and photo inspiration.

Include Post-It notes in your binder to add small notes and reminders in different categories. Post-Its come in a variety of different sizes and colors for detailed organization. I used lined notepad Post-Its, regular Post-Its, small Post-Its to make appointment corrections in my calendar, and bookmark Post-Its to make it easier to flip to certain parts of the binder. The bookmark Post-Its were very useful in further dividing folder categories. For example, in the beauty folder I put Post-It bookmarks for hair ideas, nail salons, and makeup ideas.

Once all supplies are gathered, put your binder together. Order the folders by what needs to be done first, what is most important to you, or randomly. The binder should be organized in a way that makes the most sense to you.

The binder will be undergoing additions and revisions throughout your engagement up until your wedding day, so plan on bringing it with you practically everywhere, especially in planning consultations to take notes or show pictures of ideas and preferences. Bring it to work so you can look it over and plan during breaks. Have it with you at family get-togethers to refer to answers or show visuals when people ask questions about the planning. The binder is not only an organizational tool for yourself, it will also make your wedding match exactly what you envision.

Your Lifelines: To-Do List and Calendars

After your binder is officially set up, the first thing to do is iron out a to-do list divided by months. I briefly mentioned this in the previous chapter, but here is a refresher. Figure out how many months you have to plan the wedding. Distribute the tasks to complete accordingly in two-three month segments, followed by monthly sections when three months prior, then weekly for six weeks out, and daily the final week.

Thanks to the internet, there are many wedding planning and research websites that serve as a guide and inspiration. The one I used, and my favorite, is called *The Knot* (http://theknot.com). At *The Knot*, sign up for a free account and enter in basic information about yourself, your fiancé, and your wedding details. There are an abundance of resources available on *The Knot*. It is definitely worth an afternoon exploring all the facets of the website. I will be referring to different resources *The Knot* offers throughout this book, starting with the to-do list.

For *The Knot*'s to-do list, you simply input your wedding date for the site to list and outline planning tasks by the date it should be completed. To instill a sense of urgency, it puts exclamation points next to tasks that are late or running out of time to finish. While *The Knot* to-do list is great for giving you a timeline, some of the suggestions can be unimportant or repetitive. The checklist can be customized by adding and removing tasks, but I found it easier to use *The Knot* checklist as a timeline source and create my own to-do list.

As you begin crafting your to-do list, I cannot stress how important it is to book your venue immediately with your vendors right behind. The venue for both the ceremony and reception should be booked in the first two or three weeks of planning while all vendors should be booked within the first month and a half. The earlier this is done increases the likelihood of getting all of the vendors you want without dates conflicting. As I mentioned in Chapter One, do not set a concrete date until your favorite or most important vendors tell you they are available.

The rest of the to-do list will be explained as if you have nine months to plan a wedding. I will give notes on adjustments to make depending if you have more or less time to plan.

The first three month section is for 7-9 months before the wedding. Start your to-do list with items like "Book photographer" or "Book venue." These will seem simple, but there is a lot of research and many phone calls and meetings that go into these tasks. Even though they look easy, these tasks take a lot of time. Vendors must be booked well within this time frame. Waiting until a couple of months before will cause immense stress and may result in not getting certain vendors at all, depending on the month or the day of your wedding.

If you only have a few months to plan, understand that sacrifices might be made for preferred vendors and it's possible you will have to settle for a vendor fourth or fifth on your list, especially if you are getting married in a popular wedding month.

TIP: June and September are the most popular months to get married, and the most expensive. In December, you will compete with holiday parties for venues and vendors. The months with the most availability are January, March, April, and November.

Vendors are going to take up most of the planning for this section. Brides should also start shopping for their wedding dress. This may take most of your planning time or you might find the perfect dress on your first visit to a bridal shop. While shopping, start looking at bridesmaids dresses.

The guest list also needs to be finalized in this section. The guest list will help dictate the size needed for venues and food count. Some venues will only have room for 50 people, others for 300. Only an estimated guest count is initially required by vendors, but compiling a final guest list will help with booking and creating a budget. The more guests you have, the more expensive vendors will be. Another benefit of finalizing a guest list is the ability to gather addresses early, making the invitation section much easier. These are the main tasks that need to be accomplished in the first three month planning segments.

The next segment is for 4-6 months before the wedding date. Early on, take your bridesmaids dress shopping so decisions can be made and dresses can be ordered in time for getting alterations done. This section is also the time for registering for gifts. It is done this early in case you change your mind a few (dozen) times before the wedding. Registrations need to be completely done before sending out invitations. It is a good idea to choose and order invitations at this time.

If you find you do not need much for your house, you can always choose to register for your honeymoon. When you go through a travel agent, you can have guests put money toward activities, such as a catamaran cruise or a ski tour. They can also donate money as a gift for your honeymoon. The honeymoon registry option is convenient, since the honeymoon needs to be planned during this period. Planning the honeymoon can seem overwhelming, but it can be done in one weekend if you and your fiancé commit to booking it. I will cover more about honeymoon planning in Chapter Eleven.

The last main thing that needs to be accomplished in this planning block is the décor. This may seem like something that can be accomplished closer to the wedding date. No matter how simple you think your décor is, it takes time to shop and acquire all the items needed. This is best accomplished in a section that does not have as many tasks to finish, such as this one. Décor does not necessarily have to be purchased during this period, but it should be planned at this time what you want to do.

The next planning segment is 2-3 months before the day of the wedding. This chapter has a lot of miscellaneous tasks that need to be accomplished. The first thing to do is mail your invitations. To make life easier, choose and order invitations in the previous planning section.

This is the time to shop for and buy wedding bands. If you and your fiancé want to gradually pay off your rings, then put them on layaway earlier in the engagement period. Make sure enough time is allowed to pay for the rings and get them properly sized before the wedding.

Schedule your hair and makeup appointments in this time period, including a trial run two weeks before and official appointments the day of. Don't forget to schedule appointments for your bridesmaids and flower girls.

Lingerie should be purchased during this period. This does not only mean wedding night and honeymoon items, as fun as they are to shop for! Lingerie includes any undergarment needed for the dress such as a petticoat, corset, bra, and underwear.

Dress fittings should be scheduled at the very beginning of this time frame. There should be at least two fittings, but make sure the first fitting is scheduled early enough to leave ample time for additional fittings.

There are a few miscellaneous things that need to be done with this segment. This includes:

- Final decisions on ceremony music
- Final gift registry
- Finalize and send the bridal shower guest list to Maid of Honor
- First band or DJ meeting

Now here is the biggest section: one month before. Suspense music would be appropriate here. This month is basically a laundry list of things that haven't yet been completed, along with last minute tasks that need to be accomplished. Make a checklist of everything you have not had a chance to do, and add these items:

- Order wedding favors
- Make or order guest book
- Get all accessories including veil, shoes, and jewelry

- Decide on and start getting your something old, borrowed, new, and blue
- Final dress fitting
- Dress pressing or cleaning
- Get the marriage license with your spouse along with blood tests if your state requires it
- Have your bridal shower
- Send bridal shower thank you notes (good practice for after the wedding!)
- Haircut, hair dye, hair trial
- Makeup trial
- Buy bridal party gifts
- Send rehearsal dinner invites
- Schedule rehearsal with ceremony location
- Pick up wedding rings
- Put together an emergency kit

You may have questions about some of these items, but they will be covered in future chapters.

Two weeks before the wedding is the last big segment. This is planned separately because of all the time sensitive tasks that need to be accomplished. Everything on this list should not be completed sooner than the two week mark.

The wedding dress needs to be picked up. This will most likely not be ready until two weeks prior, but if it is altered and pressed sooner, then it is okay to pick it up.

Confirm with *all* vendors that they are coming at the correct time and place. There might be specific arrival instructions to relay after talking to the ceremony and reception locations. Give all of your vendors a final guest count. Look at your payment schedules for each vendor and ensure they are getting their final payments at the right time. Some may be two weeks before, one week before, or the day of.

After speaking to all vendors (especially the photographer and the DJ), create the day of schedule to send to the bridal party, parents, and certain important people that need to be involved behind the scenes.

If you need a specific guest count and you are missing RSVPs, then it is appropriate to call those missing guests at this time to see if they are coming. I have a complicated relationship with the RSVP process, which I will cover more extensively in the next chapter.

There are a lot of tasks that need to be done after the wedding is over, such as taking down décor, packing presents, and getting the cake or dinner leftovers. Figure out who will take care of this and ask them to do the tasks.

The to-do list is probably the hardest part of your binder to set up. It is overwhelming because you have to lay out everything that needs to happen for your entire engagement period. The good news is you don't have to plan out anything in this section, only make lists that are not concrete. You can easily move tasks around month to month or week to week. Tasks can be added to the list throughout your planning, so no need to panic if you only make a skeleton list. Don't stress about this part, it is not as terrible as you think.

After you settle your to-do list, you need to either print out or buy a notebook calendar to add to your binder. Go through your deadlines and add them to the calendar. If you have any changes, you can add small Post-Its to cover certain days and rewrite the events. As soon as you have deadlines and payment dates from your vendors, add them to the calendar so you will remember to do everything on time. Include your own personal tasks, such as having lunch with the bridesmaids. The calendar was probably my favorite part of my binder and really helped keep me sane.

Getting the Party Started: Guest Lists and Invitations

The guest list is what defines the wedding. The number of guests that are invited will determine the size and scope of the reception. The more people who are invited, the more food, drinks, dessert, linens, table décor, and even the DJ will cost. However, the number of guests invited is completely up to the couple. My husband and I were on a tight budget, but our (large) families were important to us, so we sacrificed other things to be able to afford our guests. Besides, the more guests that are invited, the more presents you will get!

To start gathering guest names, make an initial list of names that come to mind. Consult with your fiancé for names. This will help begin painting a small picture of what to expect.

After this, go to parents on both sides to see what vital names you might be missing. Make it clear what size or kind of wedding you want to have. They may try to add too many distant relatives. It is perfectly okay to veto some of the names.

Once a list is put together and added to this section of the binder, gather addresses. The easiest way to manage addresses, catalog them for the future, and address envelopes are to type them on a computer. Many brides want beautiful, hand-addressed invitations. To save time (and hand cramps), print addresses on label stickers, and can still choose a cursive font if desired (make sure it is legible). This method prevents wasted envelopes on writing mistakes and allows couples to have a database of addresses for family and friends. Even if you prefer to hand-address envelopes in flowing calligraphy, typing them is a good way to save the addresses. The list should be printed off and put it in your wedding book for future reference when hand-addressing invites.

A guest list also gives the ability to order the correct number of invitations. There are many ways to order invitations. Specialty wedding invitation websites allow complete customization of paper, texture, and design. There are also printing websites, like *Vistaprint* (http://vistaprint.com), that offer premade designs with text and color customization. These sites are more affordable, but have less customization and paper type options.

TIP: When ordering invites, order at least 10 and no more than 25 more invitations and envelopes than guests. This gives you plenty of extra invitations for last minute guests and keepsakes. If you feel like you are prone to messing up addresses, make sure you order extra envelopes on top of this number.

The timeframe for sending out invitations is very specific. If your wedding is in less than three months, send invitations out *immediately*. Most guides say invitations need to be sent 8 to 12 weeks before. When I was planning my wedding, I thought (and still believe) that 12 weeks is not enough time. However, I overcorrected and sent invitations out five months before. I did this to give more time for people to respond, get an early guest count for vendors, and be less stressed the month before the wedding.

The problem with this was many people figured they had plenty of time to respond and forgot about the wedding entirely. Other people immediately RSVP'd a yes, then either forgot about the wedding or had other things come up so they could not intend.

What happened to me was over half of my guests did not respond. I had to shake people down two weeks before to see if they were coming, which I didn't like doing. I put pressure on both of our families to help me out. I ended up making guesses on who would or would not come and rounded that number for the caterer and the tables that needed to be set. The day of my wedding when I arrived to the reception, there were at least 10 empty tables. I realized people who had responded yes months ago did not show up!

Moral of the story: send invitations out at the three month mark *exactly*. This is the perfect amount of time. If I had to do it over again, I would send out a cute postcard with a fun picture of the happy couple two weeks before. I would have the postcard say how excited we are to get married and we are anxious to see the guests at the wedding. For the guests who have responded "yes," this is a perfect reminder to them that your wedding is coming up. For guests who have not responded, I would add to the postcard asking if we would see them with a contact number or email.

This leads me to my next point – do not stress over the RSVPs like I did. Yes, you do need a guest count for the caterer, bartender, desserts, DJ, and reception hall. However, it is easier to go through the list with family and guess who will and will not come. From there, get a rounded guess. If serving a plated dinner, then I wish you the best of luck getting a count.

To keep track of RSVPs, write or type a guest list out of the wedding. Write in how many people are in a party and make columns for yes and no. Fill out who is a yes or no in each party in the appropriate column. This will help keep track of the guest count. Keep your list of estimates on who may or may not come as a reference guide to the actual count.

There are also websites that help you keep track of RSVPs, even allowing guests to respond over the internet. For example, I used (http://anrsvp.com) to keep track, but there are many others as well. I even put a link to my RSVP list on my invitations for modern guests (meaning no one older than 50) to RSVP online instead of through the mail. This saves money on postage and makes responses easier to keep track of online.

In the folder, put ideas, themes, or colors desired for the invitations. Collect sample ideas from bridal magazines to put in the folder for inspiration. Figure out the wording of the invitation that best fits. There are hundreds of guides for this on the internet, so choose the wording scheme that works for you, your fiancé, and your families.

TIP: If you have created a wedding website, put this on the bottom of the invitation. I highly recommend a website. It allows the other side of the family to get to know the new addition and can be a forever keepsake. It also can include information that is difficult to fit on an invitation. It is easier and cleaner than stuffing a bunch of informative papers and directions in the envelopes. There are many free wedding website domains on the internet, including one on The Knot.

Wedding invitations are not the only thing that needs to be ordered as stationary, will also need envelopes, RSVP cards, save-the-dates, thank you cards, bridal shower invites, and more. Envelopes can be in different designs and colors than standard white to stand out in a stack of mail. A common trend with thank you cards is to put a picture of the couple on the card, either from engagement or wedding photos. Many couples are choosing to get thank you postcards to save money on stamps while being unique and creative.

Guest lists need to be created for the engagement party, bridal shower, and bachelor and bachelorette parties. These lists (with addresses) should be written down in the folder and a copy sent to the host of the parties. For the bridal shower and bachelorette, this is the Maid of Honor. For the bachelor party, it is the Best Man. The host of the party will be in charge of planning, sending invitations, and managing responses. You only need to make the guest lists in your planning binder.

The Day of Schedule should be tucked into this folder. This is tricky because your timeline for the day may be changed multiple times. Be sure to consult with your vendors on times before creating a complete schedule.

TIP: Your photographer is going to be your best friend when planning the timeline. They will let you know how much time you will need for picture taking, locations, and travel.

I Do: The Ceremony

The ceremony folder will contain everything relating to your ceremony. If you don't know where you are getting married, make a list of all potential ceremony locations of interest. Leave room for notes about the costs, times, requirements, and your impressions of each ceremony location you visit.

In this section, put a list of questions you want to ask. This can be related to costs, rules, rehearsal, or things you want to do during the ceremony. To help kick start your list, common questions include:

- Do you have a pianist for the music or a sound system?

- Do you require marriage counseling and what does it entail?

- Do you have a ceremony coordinator?

- Do you have dressing rooms for the bridal parties to get ready?

- How early can we get to the ceremony?

- Will you allow us to rehearse the night before?

Once you have chosen a location, write down their address, contact information, and rules and details about the space for future reference.

TIP: *Always choose an officiant who offers marriage counseling. Regardless how long you have been dating or living together, marriage counseling will greatly benefit your relationship and put you in the right mindset to make the lifelong commitment.*

The rest of this section should have brainstorming about what you want to do in your ceremony. If you want to write your own vows, start making drafts. Make sure you ask your officiant about their vow and ceremony requirements. Some officiants have a set of vows they require you use while others have certain things they cover during a ceremony. Make a list of what the ceremony progression will be, either by your preference or what your officiant dictates. A common progression of events is as follows:

- Welcome

- Officiant's address

- Declaration of Intent

- Vows

- Exchange of rings

- Blessing or closing remarks

- Pronouncement

Often the ceremony space will guide you on the processional, or what order everyone walks down the aisle, but make sure to write down any preferences, and pick out some scripture passages you want the ceremony to be centered around if you are having a church wedding. The scripture should be chosen as a couple. The passage you choose will be the foundation of your ceremony, and your marriage.

There are many things you can feature in your ceremony, but here are the three most popular rituals you can feature:

Unity Candle: At the beginning of the ceremony, representatives from each family (usually the mothers of the bride and groom) light two taper candles. After the vows, the couple will use the two taper candles to light a large pillar candle to represent their unity.

Unity Sand: Usually there is a table set up behind the couple with a large empty jar and two smaller jars filled with two different colors of sand. The officiant reads a statement as each person picks up a jar of sand and alternates turns filling up the empty jar. The officiant caps the jar to make a colorful keepsake from the wedding.

Wine Box: The couple places a bottle of wine from the year of their wedding along with love letters in a box. They take turns hammering a lid on the box and agree to open it at a predetermined anniversary date (such as five or ten years). The contents of the box usually vary by couple.

Besides these optional ceremony choices, there are a few other items that are commonly found in ceremonies. Many couples supply a program with the ceremony order, featured songs, and the people in the processional.

TIP: If you want to save money or time on printing programs, then make a pretty sign that is placed outside of the ceremony space, perhaps on or next to the gift table. Guests get to see it walking in and it can be a neat feature to a themed wedding. However, there are many cute and creative ceremony programs out there, such as the program being printed on paper fans for an outdoor wedding in the summer.

Also consider the flower girl baskets and petals, ring bearer pillow, transportation from the ceremony, and bubbles or some kind of confetti for guests to throw while you are walking out.

Party Time: The Reception

The location for the reception is going to be your first big hurdle after setting the date. It is very important to set up appointments at multiple reception locales and tour them before choosing one. Once you have the reception and ceremony locations decided, you can start planning the rest of the wedding.

Finding options for the reception was difficult for me. This is yet another area The Knot saved my life. The Knot has a list of reception locations in your area that users have compiled and reviewed that can be sorted by price to find one in your range.

Realize, though, that many locations have extra fees outside of the rental. There are also different rules, such as requirements to use their food services or alcohol, which can add to the price. This is why it is necessary to ask plenty of questions to get a thorough understanding of their prices, including:

- Can I see a list of estimated prices for my date?
- Can I have a written estimate?
- Does my deposit lock in the price?
- How much is the deposit and when does it have to be paid?
- What is the refund policy on deposits?
- Is the deposit credited toward the final bill?
- What time can I begin setup?
- What are all of your extra costs in writing?
- What exactly is included in my rental payment?

- Do you provide food or alcohol services and how much is it?

- Do I have to use your food or alcohol services?

- What kind of lighting and décor do you provide?

- What things can I bring in for décor? What is the limit?

- Do you have a list of preferred vendors?

- What are all of your gratuity and tax charges?

- What are the due dates for required information?

- When and how do I schedule my final walk-through?

- What are all the contingency fees?

Take notes on all of this information in your reception folder. Lay this information out in chart form for easy comparison of prices, amenities, location, contact information, and overall appearance for each reception venue. Write down the address, website, and all contact information on the chart.

Before choosing a location, factor in all of the extra costs and amenities to help decide if the location is too expensive. Request a list of preferred vendors from the location and see what discounts you can receive going through your reception location. This might save enough money to make the expense of the hall worthwhile.

The most important thing to remember is you have the power of negotiation. Reception sites want to fill up their calendar. Make it clear you are interested in the site, but are also looking at a few other places. Ask the site if they can give a discount on an amenity or include a certain amenity in the rental price. If they do, go ahead and put a deposit down for booking. To get your business, most places are willing to negotiate.

Keep a copy of the rental contract and put it in your folder in case of disputes or as a reference in case you forget the guidelines for the location. Also, get a layout of your reception hall, along with how many tables they offer and how many seats are on each table. This will be helpful when you have a guest count to plan the layout of the reception. Some locations will have pre-set layouts while others will let you completely customize the hall. A layout will help you figure out how much décor you will need and how to display. This will be discussed in the next chapter.

Looking Good: Décor

The décor section of the wedding binder is going to be filled with notes, shopping lists, brainstorming, photos, sketches, and receipts. Lots of receipts.

Maybe you have an idea of what kind of décor you want or have no idea where to start. First, define your colors for the wedding. This will help you find a starting ground or give you a theme idea. In my case, my favorite color is sapphire and I love the colors of autumn (and my husband and I met in autumn). So I had fall leaves everywhere with blue accents accompanying them.

After figuring out your colors, get a bunch of different ideas from the internet. Wedding websites like *The Knot* have inspiration pages. However, Pinterest (http://pinterest.com) helped me the most. Search "wedding" and it will come up with hundreds of décor ideas. If you see something you like, Pin it to your board for future reference and visit the user's board for more ideas. Print out inspiring pictures and put them in your décor folder.

Start by making a list of décor needed for the ceremony before starting the reception. If you don't have a vision already in place, don't worry about trying to find décor. No need to fill the space up with stuff, especially if it is beautiful on its own. Décor that couples often choose include aisle runners, ribbons for pews, flowers for pews, flowers on stage, candles on stage, or petals scattered on aisle and stage.

TIP: Décor is not needed for the ceremony. Not even an aisle runner. Stick to flower girl petals, programs, a unity candle, unity sand, and other items strictly related to religion or union. The reason for reception décor is because a reception hall is usually a blank canvas to build upon.

Décor goes beyond centerpieces. Consider the gift table, dessert table, buffet table if choosing this dinner option, and any extra tables you want out for games or other cute décor pieces. To organize all of my ideas, I made a list for all of the décor and fun touches I wanted at my reception. I narrowed down the list and added new ideas over the months of my engagement until I had a final list of ideas.

I had so many separate pieces to my décor that I found it helpful to make sketches of each table's décor. It helped me visualize the space and ensure I didn't miss anything when shopping. Once you have a final list of ideas, it's time to use the reception layout guide from chapter five. Place all of your décor in its proper place in the reception hall. Use the layout and guest count to figure out how many tables need to be out, which is how to figure out how many centerpieces to order.

List of all the pieces of décor to buy. Create a master list and spend time researching where to find the best or most affordable pieces to match your ideas. If you have a clear idea of what you want, separate your shopping list by store to make the shopping easier.

This folder should be very organized so not worrying about getting an extra candle or missing flowers the night before or day of the wedding. Keep all the purchase receipts in this folder in case you change your mind and need to make returns. If ordering flowers for your décor, the receipt may be needed if your order is wrong when delivered.

Who Makes the Wedding Happen: Vendors

Oh boy. The vendors. One of the most complicated things to coordinate for your wedding. Every vendor you want needs to be available on the same day, which we discussed in earlier chapters. This folder will contain vendor information when researching options, contracts, payment plans and due dates, and other details for each vendor you hire. Examples of vendors for hire include caterer, alcohol, cake, florists, DJ or band, photographer, and videographer.

Selecting these vendors is up to personal preference for the kind of look, mood, style, and budget you need for your wedding. Here we will discuss what to do after selecting your vendors and what information to add to your folder. To be ultra-organized, give each vendor their own folder in your binder, but I just threw all of them together. In this book, however, we will break down the tips by vendor.

Have the payment due dates for each vendor in this folder so payments are not forgotten. Trust me, this is very easy to do. Most vendors require their final payment either two weeks before, one week before, or the day of. This is on top of deposits and other payments leading up to the day. It can all get very confusing, so put the payment schedules for each vendor in this folder.

TIP: Consider making payment due date marks in your calendar section, discussed in chapter two. Also make sure to get a business card from every vendor and tape it in the folder for easy contact reference.

Caterer

The most important thing needed in the vendor folder for the caterer is a phone number and email in case you change your mind on the menu, adjust your guest count, and ask about expanding or reducing your food items. The contact information is your best friend.

Look through the menu options and make a list of your favorites to order for your taste test. Give yourself plenty of choices. Even after you and your fiancé have selected your menu options, keep the second and third favorites noted after the tasting in case you change your mind.

Make a memo of the price per head and guest count so you can figure out how much it will cost.

TIP: My caterer gave me some outstanding advice that I will pass on to you. When getting your guest count for the caterer, do not tally children who are under 2 because they won't eat enough to make a difference in serving sizes. Also, any kids under 8 should only be counted as half a person. This will save you a lot of money, and extra food, for your catering.

Alcohol

This section depends on whether or not your reception venue supplies alcohol and if they require the use of their alcohol. If they don't but allow you to hire an alcohol provider, then include a space for prices and contact information. If they have a bar, but let you bring in your own alcohol, I suggest buying your own. Then hire a separate bartender or ask a friend to do it (if they are licensed and/or your reception allows it).

I thought my hall allowed me to bring in my own alcohol, so I shopped around and calculated how much alcohol I would need to buy for 150 people. I found out that I wasn't allowed to bring in my own, but I still kept this well-rounded supply list I created. So, if you are allowed to bring in your own alcohol, then here is a guide for everything needed:

- 2 kegs
- 3 handles rum
- 1 handle gin

- 3 handles tequila
- 3 bottles Crown Royal
- 3 bottles champagne
- 2 bottles Pinto Grigio
- 2 bottles Chardonnay
- 2 bottles Menot
- 2 liters Coke
- 2 liters Diet Coke
- 2 liters Sprite
- 2 liters tonic water
- 1 jug cranberry juice
- 1 jug orange juice
- 1 jug lemonade
- 2 bottles margarita mix

Cake

Sometimes your caterer will offer bakery services. If you like that all-in-one option, you can do that, but I recommend a standalone baker for your cake. Look through the baker's portfolio for cake ideas. In the binder, put cake photos from magazines or the internet for inspiration and bring them to the meeting with the baker. Make sure you know the rough number of people the cake needs to feed.

A popular trend at weddings is to pass out cupcakes to guests instead of slices of cake. Create a cupcake tier that mimics the look of a cake or just have them in boxes to pass out. If you still want the cake cutting tradition, just order a small cake that serves you, your bridal party, and immediate family along with cupcakes for your guests.

TIP: Don't forget to order the small top tier of the cake for your one year anniversary. Assign someone to box it up at the end of the night and freeze it.

Floral

Before ordering flowers, first decide how many flowers you want. There are bridesmaids bouquets and your bouquet. You may also want boutonnieres, flower petals for the flower girls, petals for the tables, corsages for the mothers and grandmothers, floral centerpieces for the tables, flowers for the pews, and bouquets on the ceremony stage if desired. Once arrangement decisions are completed, choose what kinds of flowers to feature and place pictures of them in your binder.

Make a list and gather pictures of the kinds of flowers wanted in your flower arrangements. Also gather pictures of bouquet and centerpiece arrangements you love and want emulated at your wedding. Florists love to see visuals of what is desired for so they can best achieve the visualized look.

If you have no idea what flowers you might want, the florist will figure it out. Florists will ask you all of the questions about the theme, colors, and overall mood and style of the wedding. They will then share pictures of flowers they think will fit or create small, simple arrangements to show how certain flowers and colors look together.

Keep track of your inspiration pictures and flowers selected for your arrangements in the binder.

TIP: Flowers are beautiful, but can be expensive. If you have floral arranging skills, you can buy flowers wholesale in bulk and create your own bouquets and centerpieces. This is also a fun bonding activity that can be done with your bridal party and family. Fake flowers are a great option for arrangements if you are on a tight budget, especially with sales at hobby and craft stores.

Music

Whether hiring a DJ or band, keep a section of the vendor folder reserved for them. For a band, keep a copy of the band's playlist and make a list of favorite songs they play. They need to receive your first dance song so they can perform it. The band may also need to announce certain events at your reception, so keep in contact with them during planning to lay out a reception schedule with them. The band may require a face to face meeting to plan the night.

For a DJ, a face to face meeting with them is best so the DJ can get a feel for the kind of couple you and your fiancé are. DJs focus more on the fun, dance club vibe while the band is elegant and authentic. DJs need to understand a couple's personality to customize the night and will be able to play better music selections for you and the theme of your wedding. DJs will feature more games and fun activities to do during the reception, such as the dollar dance and garter and bouquet toss. At the meeting, work with your DJ to schedule the order of events for the reception.

Make sure to create a "must play" and "do not play" list for both the DJ and the band.

TIP: For a memorable reception, look up alternative ways to do traditions, such as the dollar dance or garter toss. Also look up new reception games (like the Shoe Game) to add some uniqueness to your reception.

Photographer

The photographer section should include some of your favorite poses from other weddings or couples shoots. Make a list of must have moments you want captured. Some photographers hate this while others welcome it. Ask your photographer if they would like to refer to your list of preferred photo captures.

This part of the binder should also be used to brainstorm cute ideas for your wedding photos or engagement session. For example, you could get a newspaper the day of your wedding and get pictures taken of all rings circling the date or have cute signs for people in the bridal party to hold.

TIP: Always do an engagement photo session before the wedding day. This will help you and your fiancé get comfortable being intimate in front of the camera. Using the same photographer for the engagement and wedding gives a chance to build chemistry with him or her.

The photographer is going to be your greatest asset when creating the timeline for the day. Consult with him or her before setting up the time for the ceremony and reception or making the invitations. They will let you know the amount of time needed for the bridal party photos, both before and after the ceremony. This will help you schedule hair and makeup, the time to arrive at the ceremony, and when the reception should begin. Don't forget to factor in driving time.

TIP: Photo booths are becoming very popular for receptions. They are a great way to entertain guests before you arrive and during the reception when they are done eating or want a break from dancing. You can get a photo booth from your photographer, an independent vendor, or your reception site. If you get a booth from your photographer, make sure that one photographer out of your team is not taken away to maintain the photo booth. The operator of the booth needs to be a separate photographer.

Videographer

Often your videographer will be a subset of your photographer, or your photographer can recommend one they work well with so that your photographer and videographer don't get in the way of each other and miss important shots. In your folder, make a list of the must have moments your videographer needs to capture. Keep a list of the different packages and their prices in case you decide to upgrade or downgrade.

In the vendor folder, complete a postcard with the phone number of all the vendors. This keeps the contact info all in one place for easy access and should be with your Maid of Honor the day of the wedding. Problems do happen, so it's important all numbers are conveniently available so your Maid of Honor can call the baker if the cake isn't on time or the florist if you are missing a boutonniere. The card should also have contact info of VIPs, again, just in case. This includes the bride and groom, bridal party, parents, officiant, reception site manager, and anyone with authority behind the scenes.

TOP SECRET: Dress, Outfits, and Wedding Bands

The section of your binder for the dress and other outfits is going to be very visual. Insert cutouts from bridal magazines and print pictures off the internet for the dress, the groom's outfit, and bridal party outfits. These images will serve as your inspiration and help bridal shops find the perfect outfits for your special people.

TIP: Have color swatches for your overall wedding colors and choose the one for the bridesmaid dresses and groomsmen ties or vests. Every vendor is going to want a swatch for your colors, so make sure to have a bunch on hand.

Many pictures of your dream dress in the binder will help consultants in bridal shops find a gown that matches your expectations. If you don't have a clear image of what you want for your dress, then getting picture inspiration is absolutely necessary. Buy bridal magazines and cut out dresses. Go to major bridal dressmaker's websites (even ones you are not able to afford) and print off dresses you love. *Pinterest* is another great place for wedding dress inspiration. *Pinterest* may get teased for the intense wedding boards users have, but it really is a goldmine of wedding ideas. If at any point you don't have an idea for your wedding, go to *Pinterest* and your problems will be solved.

When shopping for your dress, show the shopper consultants your collection of dress inspiration. They can go through their inventory based off your ideas and find dresses that match. Once you find your dress, have your Maid of Honor or mom take pictures of you wearing it. Print them out and put them in the binder. This may freak you out because your fiancé could see it (outlaw him from touching the binder!), but *everyone* is going to ask to see your dress. Some vendors even insist on seeing it so they can help design their services. With all of these requests, it is convenient to keep pictures of your dress in the binder for easy reference. This is especially helpful when people ask you to describe it with your fiancé around.

While looking for your dress, seek additional inspiration for your bridesmaids dress style. I am an advocate of letting bridesmaids choose their own dresses, especially if they are paying for them. You can set parameters, like color, whether they are all the same or different style, and their length. The dresses need to be ordered and paid for in full by five months before the wedding. This leaves time for the dresses to come in and alterations completed.

TIP: For bridesmaid dress inspiration, refer to David's Bridal's magazine. Even if you have no desire to go there (many brides have an aversion to the chain, but I got my dress there and everyone loved it and were shocked to learn it was from David's Bridal), their bridesmaid dress selection is huge and can provide a lot of ideas. Their bridesmaid collection has different length options and a palette of color options, plus it folds out, making it convenient to place in your binder and unfold for the bridesmaid opinions.

If your groom-to-be is involved in the planning, let him pick his own suit for the wedding. He only needs a swatch color while shopping. Otherwise, compile photos of different kinds of suits that he will look *amazing* wearing. Even if your guy insists on saying, "Whatever you want," he will probably start making decisions when you both go suit shopping. It is good to compile images to get an idea of his style and the groomsmen's look.

Included in this folder is all accessories for the outfits, as pictures or simply listed. This can include the veil, shoes for everyone in the bridal party, petticoat or bustier, garter, jewelry for the bride and bridesmaids, and anything else you want to add to your outfits. For men, this can be the pocket square, ties or bow ties, unique shoes, hats, and more. Make a checklist in this section with links or pictures of ideas, along with price comparisons.

Lastly, in this section should be research on alteration shops and dress cleaning and pressing locations. Sometimes bridal shops where the dress is purchased will offer alterations, but read reviews first. For example, I bought my dress at David's Bridal and *loved* it, but I read reviews that said they were overpriced for alterations and messed up a lot of dresses. So I found another store to do it. The best way to find an alteration store is through referrals. Also make sure the alteration shop can work with your dress material and style.

The dress will require at least two alteration appointments. The first will be making decisions about whether to shorten the length, tighten or loosen the straps, take the dress in or let it out, and how the train will be bustled. The second alteration will be a check to make sure everything looks okay and fits well. If more corrections need to be made, then a third appointment is scheduled.

For cleaning, pressing, and preserving, ask around your area for dry cleaners who specialize in wedding dresses. The person completing the alterations may have a recommendation.

TIP: Get your dress cleaned before the wedding. It will be tossed around an alteration shop and probably dragged along the floor. Pressing is overpriced at dry cleaners, however, so I recommend getting a hand steamer and steaming your dress the morning of the wedding.

As usual, keep all receipts in this folder. This is especially important for rented suits since they need to be returned immediately to avoid a late fee. The receipt will include the required return date.

Even though they are not necessarily top secret, wedding bands should go in this folder (mainly for lack of a better place for them). You and your fiancé should visit jewelry stores and take notes on the wedding bands you love. Start with the shop where your fiancé got your engagement ring, there might be a band that matches the ring. It's good to have all insurance and guarantee information from the same shop. The shop may also have a matching band for your fiancé if you want your rings to match.

In the folder, you can research unique metal options for men's wedding bands if matching rings is not a concern. For example, my husband is a firefighter and chose a tungsten ring because it does not scratch, smudge, or break. Most jewelry shops offer these unique materials and have sample rings for men to try, since most can only be sized one time. This makes it important to get accurate sizing. Remember to account for finger swelling and shrinking in the summer and winter respectively. There are also different widths and color accents for men's rings.

Ask the jeweler how long it takes to size the band once it is paid in full. This will assist planning when to pick up the rings and when to have them paid. Keep receipts for the layaway amount, the full payment amount, and a business card for your associate in the folder. Also make sure to receive care or insurance guarantees in writing for future reference.

Beauty: Hair, Makeup, and Nails

There are many different beauty treatment (and spa treatment) options before the wedding to look and feel beautiful. Use the folder to make a list of all the beauty treatments you want to receive and how much they are for budgeting.

There are some common beauty treatments many brides want specifically for the wedding. Within days of the wedding, consider getting your nails and toenails done with your bridesmaids and mothers of the bride and groom. This is a fun bonding experience and you have the excuse of "needing" it for the wedding.

For your hair, plan to schedule two appointments with the salon of choice for your formal day hair. Two weeks before, have your hair cut (and possibly highlighted) by the same hairdresser that will be styling your up-do. She will be able to cut it a certain way to match your wedding hair. In that same appointment, you will do a trial for your wedding hair.

Make sure to research and print different wedding hair styles you love and put them in the binder to show the hairdresser. They like seeing pictures so they can create the perfect hairstyle for your tastes. The second appointment will be the day of the wedding with your bridesmaids and flower girls. Once again, have pictures in your binder of the hairstyles for your bridal party.

Often the salon where your hair is done will offer wedding makeup. You can have them do the makeup for everyone with the same two appointments above or ask a talented friend for help. Regardless, find some eye shadow palettes and shading you want and put the ideas in the binder to show your makeup artist.

Present Time: Registry, VIP Gifts, and Miscellaneous

This folder is mainly for gift-related tasks. The gift information will not take up much room, so add miscellaneous things to this folder or start a new folder if preferred.

You and your fiancé can go to stores and physically reserve gift registries, but I found it easier to gradually add gifts online. I ended up changing our registry a few times a month leading right up to a couple of weeks before the wedding. This same list will help you purchase gifts not received using wedding gift cards and money.

As I mentioned in chapter two, if you don't have a lot you need for your house, you can register for your honeymoon instead. This means people will either donate money for the honeymoon or buy an activity for the newlyweds to enjoy on the honeymoon. To choose this option, go through a travel agent who can set up a registry website.

Put a final copy of your registry in this folder. As you receive gifts, you will see some people do not go through your registry to buy the gift which means the item is still listed as available on your registry. Keep track of your gifts and mark things as filled online so you don't get duplicate gifts and make unnecessary returns.

For all parties, have someone (usually your Maid of Honor) make a list of gifts you open and who they are from. Place this in the folder to use as an easy reference when writing thank you cards.

This is a good section to put gift ideas for your VIPs. Usually, this means bridesmaids, groomsmen, parents of the bride and groom, and anyone else who was a big help in wedding planning. For example, my aunt is a wedding coordinator for her church and knows *everything* about weddings. I was constantly asking for her advice and opinion, plus all of my cousins were in the wedding. My husband's grandmother lives near us and was a huge help whenever I needed something printed or opinions on different things. I gave them each a personalized gift to say thank you for all of their help.

Give gifts to anyone who greatly helped you with planning and made your life easier. The people in your life are doing everything they can to make your day special and less stressful, so find a meaningful way to say thank you.

This folder should be filled with any other miscellaneous information that doesn't fit anywhere else, such as extra receipts, random brainstorming lists, or sketches. In my folder, I put a bunch of tips I gathered from people and the internet about the big day. For example:

TIP: *Put baby powder on your inner thighs so they don't chaff when you inevitably start sweating.*

I included a list for the emergency kit contents in this folder. I highly recommend an emergency kit because you never know what is going to happen. Even if only one thing in the kit is useful, it will be worth it. There are many wedding emergency kit lists online you can use as a starting point, but make sure to add other things you personally will need. For example, my husband has allergies and asthma, so I made sure he had his medication with him.

This folder can also have anything else you want to do for your engagement period, such as get a couple's massage or have a fun day out with your bridesmaids.

Newlywed Time: Honeymoon

Yes, there is a lot to plan for the wedding alone without having to worry about the honeymoon. But you and your fiancé need to dedicate a weekend to figuring out what you want to do. There are three easy ways to plan a honeymoon:

Groupon: *Groupon* (http://groupon.com) is a great way to get a dream destination for your honeymoon at an affordable price. It can also be easier to plan if you snatch an all-inclusive *Groupon* with a flight included. Purchase two of the selected *Groupon*, one for you and one for your fiancé, then contact the agency who put the deal up. From there, you can arrange all travel details. The only problem with *Groupon* is you can't purchase too far in advance for a deal in your timeframe, and sometimes the dates available do not match when you want to take your honeymoon after your wedding. If traveling out of the country, make sure you and your fiancé have passports well before your wedding.

Travel Agent: If there is room in your budget, a travel agent is the best option for planning your honeymoon, especially if you find that one that does not charge fees. They will interview extensively and find the best locations based on your interests or honeymoon goals. If you don't need a registry for home items, a travel agent can help you establish a honeymoon registry as mentioned in previous chapters. Guests can donate money to your honeymoon or can buy honeymoon activities.

DIY: This is the most labor intensive option when planning a honeymoon. You have to find a location, research hotels, plan activities, and figure out travel arrangements. If you love planning travel or have experience planning vacations, you can easily do it yourself. However, if you don't have a lot of experience planning the vacations, get help from someone who is a frequent traveler or has been to your honeymoon location. They will help you find better deals, better hotels, and better travel arrangements.

TIP: *If the budget is tight, consider vacation destinations that are close to home. You don't have to choose a typical honeymoon location, like Hawaii, Florida, or Cancun. Consider a popular lake, smaller beaches in Texas or Louisiana, a nearby ski resort, a bed and breakfast, or a spa-focused hotel.* Google *and* TripAdvisor (http://tripadvisor.com) *are useful when looking for these locations.*

This section of the wedding binder should have all of the contents in an easy-to-remove folder so you can pack it in your honeymoon suitcase. Everything related to your honeymoon should be placed in this folder, including:

- Brainstorming places to go
- Hotels with their reviews and amenities
- Rental car prices and options
- Flight prices and options
- Map of locale
- Travel dates and departure/arrival times
- Travel day schedules
- Payment plans
- Activities and restaurants
- Hotel information, including contact, location, directions from the airport, meal options, and room details
- Receipt for reservation of hotel, flight, rental car, etc.
- Packing lists for you and your fiancé
- Business card from the travel agent
- Plans for pets or children
- House shut down checklist
- House-sitter information

- Copies of schedules for someone at home in case of emergencies (such as your parents)
- Health or travel insurance information
- Driver's license copies
- Medication packing list and doctor's office phone number
- Emergency contact information

This folder should be carried with you in your carry-on or purse so it is easily accessible.

The Number One Rule: Keeping Up with the Binder of Insanity

When you begin this binder, you *have* to keep up with it to make its purpose effective. Bring your binder with you *everywhere*. Wedding meetings, work, family get-togethers, in the car when you go shopping, everywhere. You never know when you are going to find time to plan or when someone will want to see what you are working on. At nearly every family get-together, I was asked about the planning and could easily pull out my binder to show off what they were asking. The binder will make vendor meetings 50x faster and easier. Vendors will greatly appreciate your organization.

TIP: After the wedding is over, use your binder notes and memories of your experience to review your vendors. This is an important step. There were many couples who reviewed the vendors you researched and helped you make decisions on who to hire. You should return the favor and give credit to the amazing people who worked tirelessly to give you a dream wedding.

Keep every paper related to the wedding in the binder, including all receipts, contracts, and billing plans. If there is a dispute, confusion, or clarification, it will be easy to find the materials you need, solve the problem quickly, and experience minimal stress. The binder should be with you or your VIPs the entire day of the wedding for easy reference in case of problems.

After the wedding is over, don't throw away your binder. It is a scrapbook, a time capsule from the year you were married. It is something you can look back on fondly (and with supreme relief that you are done planning) and show your children.

In fact, while you are planning you should add a folder to the back of your binder to store keepsakes. For example, the morning after the wedding I woke up before my brand-spanking-new husband in our hotel room. I wandered around our suite and found a pad of paper with the hotel's name printed on the letterhead. I drew a pretty calligraphy message on the pad and took it with me, along with the pen. There are a bunch of cutesy keepsakes I collected during our engagement and after our wedding that I put in the binder.

Store the binder with cards received from guests at the wedding and other parties, extra invitations, marriage license, and anything else special from the wedding. Not only is your binder going to save your life while planning, it becomes extraordinarily special afterwards.

For more wedding planning tips, visit my blog "Wedding Planning Advice Your Binder Can't Hold" at
http://weddingplanningbinder.blogspot.com/
Connect with me online on Twitter at http://twitter.com/HS_Writing
Visit my website at http://hswriting.com for more works and writing services.

Special thanks to my mom, who slaved away editing this book for me (while working two jobs) so I could publish it in time for my one year engagement anniversary. Not only has she always encouraged my writing since I was four and wrote a story about a big fish I caught, but she works tirelessly to make me a better writer.

I also have to thank my husband who encouraged me to write this book. He has supported my desire to write full time from the first time he learned that's what I wanted to do. He works hard as a firefighter and paramedic to help me achieve my dream and I never take it for granted. He is incredibly smart and takes the time to read my writing, offer amazing content suggestions, and help me grow.

About the Author

Heather Waugh (formerly Heather Hobbs) met her husband in 2010 when he visited his cousin at the University of Missouri. His cousin happened to be Heather's roommate. They hit it off and were engaged January 16th, 2013 and married September 7th of the same year. Heather has a degree in creative writing and works full time as a freelance writer. When her husband encouraged her to write a book about her crazy way of organizing the wedding, she went for it. She lives in the suburbs of Kansas City, MO with her husband and her little girl dog-child Charley.